U.S. PRESIDENTS

D0103047

The
United States Presidents

ANDREW JACKSON

ABDO Publishing Company

Megan M. Gunderson

visit us at
www.abdopublishing.com

Published by ABDO Publishing Company, 8000 West 78th Street, Edina, Minnesota 55439.
Copyright © 2009 by Abdo Consulting Group, Inc. International copyrights reserved in all
countries. No part of this book may be reproduced in any form without written permission from the
publisher. The Checkerboard Library™ is a trademark and logo of ABDO Publishing Company.

Printed in the United States.

Cover Photo: Getty Images
Interior Photos: Alamy p. 18; AP Images pp. 15, 21; Corbis pp. 5, 13; Corbis, detail image p. 17;
    Getty Images p. 11; iStockphoto pp. 19, 32; Library of Congress pp. 23, 27, 28, 29; National
    Archives p. 24; North Wind p. 9

Editor: Heidi M.D. Elston
Art Direction & Cover Design: Neil Klinepier
Interior Design: Neil Klinepier

Library of Congress Cataloging-in-Publication Data

Gunderson, Megan M., 1981-
 Andrew Jackson / Megan M. Gunderson.
    p. cm. -- (The United States presidents)
 Includes index.
 ISBN 978-1-60453-459-7
 1. Jackson, Andrew, 1767-1845--Juvenile literature. 2. Presidents--United States--Biography--
Juvenile literature. I. Title.

 E382.G86 2009
 973.5'6092--dc22
 [B]

                                        2008030959

CONTENTS

ANDREW JACKSON

Andrew Jackson was the seventh president of the United States. He was the first president to come from a poor family. Because of this, many people liked Jackson. They felt he represented the common man.

Growing up in South Carolina, Jackson had a difficult childhood. At age 13, he joined the **militia** to fight in the **American Revolution**.

Jackson later established a successful law practice. Then, he became a leader in politics. During the **War of 1812**, Jackson proved he was a strong soldier. He became a national hero.

In 1828, Jackson was elected president. While president, he fought against the abuse of states' rights. Jackson also spoke out against the Bank of the United States.

Meanwhile, President Jackson and other leaders broke promises made to Native Americans. They forced many tribes to leave their land and move west.

Jackson was president for two terms. He then retired to his Tennessee plantation. From there, he continued to support his fellow **Democrats**. Jackson was devoted to **democracy**. He is remembered as a true representative of the people of the United States.

TIMELINE

1767 - On March 15, Andrew Jackson was born in the Waxhaw settlement in South Carolina.

1780 - Jackson joined the militia and began fighting in the American Revolution.

1787 - In North Carolina, Jackson became a lawyer.

1791 - Jackson married Rachel Donelson Robards.

1796 - Jackson attended the convention that wrote the Tennessee state constitution; he was elected to the U.S. House of Representatives.

1797 - Jackson was elected to the U.S. Senate.

1798 - Jackson became a Tennessee Supreme Court judge.

1806 - Jackson killed Charles Dickinson in a duel.

1814 - During the War of 1812, Jackson won the Battle of Horseshoe Bend in Alabama.

1815 - Jackson won the Battle of New Orleans and became a national hero.

1821 - President James Monroe appointed Jackson military governor of Florida.

1823 - Jackson was reelected to the U.S. Senate.

1828 - Rachel Jackson died on December 22.

1829 - On March 4, Jackson became the seventh U.S. president.

1830 - Jackson signed the Indian Removal Act.

1832 - Jackson vetoed a bill to renew the Bank of the United States; Jackson was reelected president.

1845 - On June 8, Andrew Jackson died.

DID YOU KNOW?

President Andrew Jackson is featured on the U.S. $20 bill.

After Jackson's inauguration, a crowd caused trouble at the White House. They broke china, ruined furniture, and spilled punch. Jackson escaped the chaos and spent his first night as president in a hotel!

On January 30, 1835, Richard Lawrence attempted to assassinate President Jackson. This was the first time someone had tried to kill a U.S. president. Luckily, both of Lawrence's guns misfired and Jackson was unhurt.

FRONTIER CHILDHOOD

On March 15, 1767, Andrew Jackson was born in the Waxhaw settlement in South Carolina. At this time, South Carolina was a British colony. Andrew's parents had moved there from Ireland in 1765. Andrew's father was also named Andrew. He died shortly before Andrew was born. Andrew's mother was Elizabeth Hutchinson Jackson. She worked as a housekeeper. Andrew had two older brothers, Hugh and Robert.

As a young boy, Andrew picked fights and had a bad temper. However, he also protected younger children. He taught them to shoot rifles, fish, race, and wrestle.

Andrew learned to read books. Yet he was not very interested in school. Elizabeth wanted Andrew to become a minister. But he did not want this, either. Soon, the **American Revolution** interrupted Andrew's schooling.

FAST FACTS

BORN - March 15, 1767
WIFE - Rachel Donelson Robards (1767–1828)
CHILDREN - None
POLITICAL PARTY - Democrat
AGE AT INAUGURATION - 61
YEARS SERVED - 1829–1837
VICE PRESIDENTS - John C. Calhoun, Martin Van Buren
DIED - June 8, 1845, age 78

8

Andrew's birthplace was near the border of South Carolina and North Carolina.

JOINING THE FIGHT

The **American Revolution** reached the Waxhaw area in 1780. Andrew and his family helped tend the wounded. The same year, Andrew and Robert joined the **militia**. In August, they participated in the Battle of Hanging Rock in South Carolina.

In spring 1781, British soldiers captured Andrew, Robert, and other colonists. While captured, Andrew refused to clean a British officer's boots. For this, the officer slashed Andrew's arm and head with a sword. Robert also refused the officer. He was seriously injured as well.

The wounded boys were then forced to march to a prison. There, Andrew and Robert became sick with **smallpox**. Elizabeth secured their rescue. They were traded for British prisoners held in Waxhaw.

After the long trip back home, Robert died. Andrew was very sick, but his mother nursed him back to health. Then, she left to care for other sick prisoners. Elizabeth soon died of **cholera**. Andrew's brother Hugh had also died during the war.

The British officer's attack permanently scarred Andrew's head and arm.

At 14, Andrew was alone. He tried living with relatives and learning the saddle business. But he was not happy. At 16, Andrew inherited money from his grandfather. He quickly wasted the money. Then, Andrew briefly went back to school. He even tried teaching, but he did not like it.

TENNESSEE LAWYER

In 1784, Jackson went to Salisbury, North Carolina. There, he studied law. He worked very hard. In 1787, Jackson became a lawyer.

The following year, Jackson moved west of the Appalachian Mountains to Nashville. This region of North Carolina would soon be the new state of Tennessee. At the time, this was as far west as the colonies reached. The land was wild, like Jackson! There, he began a successful law practice.

In Nashville, Jackson lived in a boardinghouse. It was owned by the Donelson family. There, he met Rachel Donelson Robards. They fell in love and were married in 1791.

Five years later, Jackson bought a plantation near Nashville. He called it Hunter's Hill and built a house there. Mrs. Jackson developed Hunter's Hill into a successful plantation.

The Jacksons did not have any children of their own. However, they adopted Rachel's nephew in 1809. He took the name Andrew Jackson Jr. They also raised other nephews, including Andrew Jackson Donelson.

Rachel Jackson

A NEW POLITICIAN

In 1796, Jackson began his political career. First, he attended the convention that wrote the Tennessee state **constitution**. Then, Jackson was elected to the U.S. House of Representatives. He was Tennessee's first representative.

Jackson refused reelection. So, he left Congress on March 4, 1797. Jackson then returned home. However, he was elected to the U.S. Senate at the end of the year. He resigned his seat in 1798. That year, Jackson became a Tennessee **Supreme Court** judge.

After six years, Jackson went back to work on his plantation. That year, he sold Hunter's Hill and purchased a new plantation. The Hermitage was also near Nashville.

Meanwhile, Jackson became known for fighting in **duels**. A lawyer named Charles Dickinson insulted Mrs. Jackson. So in 1806, Jackson challenged him to a duel. Dickinson was killed, and Jackson was shot near the heart. The bullet stayed in his chest for the rest of his life.

Hermitage *means "private retreat." Jackson's original name for this home was Rural Retreat.*

THE WAR OF 1812

When the **War of 1812** began, Jackson joined the fight. He had been elected major general of the Tennessee **militia** in 1802. Now, Jackson led his men in many big battles in the South. The men soon called their tough leader "Old Hickory." This is because hickory is one of the hardest, toughest kinds of wood.

At the time, many Native Americans were angry with the U.S. government. American settlers were taking over their land. So, they fought with Great Britain against the United States.

Jackson faced Creek Native Americans in several battles. On March 27, 1814, Jackson and the Tennessee militia won an important victory. They defeated Creeks at the Battle of Horseshoe Bend in Alabama.

This victory earned Jackson a promotion to major general in the U.S. Army. Now, he was in charge of soldiers in Tennessee, Missouri, and Louisiana.

General Jackson and his men faced cold winter weather and a lack of food. Still, Jackson strongly led his men to victory against the Creeks.

WAR HERO

The **War of 1812** continued. So after his promotion, Jackson was sent to defend the city of New Orleans, Louisiana. There, he added to his group of soldiers. Free African Americans and even pirates joined him! Other new volunteers were Tennessee and Kentucky riflemen and planters.

The Battle of New Orleans

Today, a statue of Jackson stands in Jackson Square in New Orleans, Louisiana.

On January 8, 1815, Jackson triumphed again in the Battle of New Orleans. Nearly 2,000 British soldiers were hurt or killed. The Americans lost just six men, and only ten were wounded. This great victory made Jackson a war hero. Afterward, he returned home to the Hermitage.

In December 1817, President James Monroe gave Jackson new orders. Jackson went to defend Georgia settlers along the border with Spanish Florida. There, Seminole Native Americans were attacking.

This conflict became known as the First Seminole War. In 1818, Jackson marched into Florida. He captured Pensacola and Saint Marks.

In 1821, the United States gained control of Florida. President Monroe then appointed Jackson military governor of the territory. At the end of the year, Jackson resigned. Then in 1823, the Tennessee legislature reelected Jackson to the U.S. Senate. He served two years before resigning.

Meanwhile, Jackson decided to run for president. In the 1824 election, he received 99 electoral votes. John Quincy Adams received 84 and William H. Crawford received 41. Henry Clay won 37. No candidate had won a majority. So, the U.S. House of Representatives had to choose the winner.

Clay threw his support behind Adams, who won the election. Then, Adams appointed Clay **secretary of state**. Jackson felt Clay had supported Adams so they could both get into office.

This incident helped form the Jacksonian **Democracy** movement. Jackson and his supporters felt the voices of the people had not been heard. Jackson vowed to fight for the American people.

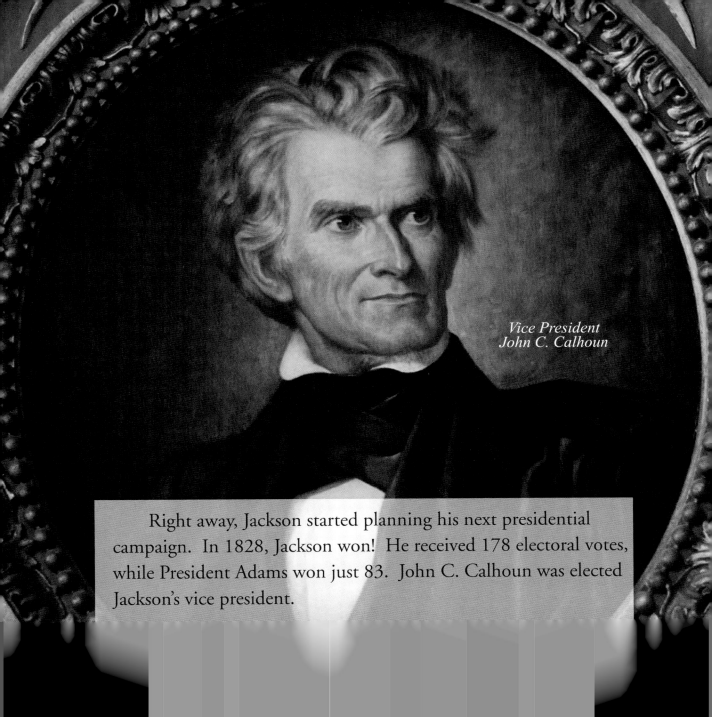

Vice President
John C. Calhoun

Right away, Jackson started planning his next presidential campaign. In 1828, Jackson won! He received 178 electoral votes, while President Adams won just 83. John C. Calhoun was elected Jackson's vice president.

PRESIDENT JACKSON

Shortly after the election, tragedy struck Jackson's life. On December 22, 1828, Rachel Jackson died. Jackson was very sad. He blamed his wife's death on his political opponents. During the campaign, they had spread terrible rumors about Mrs. Jackson.

On March 4, 1829, Jackson was **inaugurated** the seventh U.S. president. People came to the White House to celebrate their hero. The crowds were so large Jackson had to escape through a side door!

Jackson's niece Emily Donelson acted as White House hostess. Andrew Jackson Jr.'s wife, Sarah Yorke Jackson, also served as hostess.

As president, Jackson often sought advice from outside his **cabinet**. This small group of friends included politicians and newspaper editors. They became known as the Kitchen Cabinet.

PRESIDENT JACKSON'S CABINET

FIRST TERM
MARCH 4, 1829–MARCH 4, 1833

- **STATE** – Martin Van Buren
  Edward Livingston (from May 24, 1831)
- **TREASURY** – Samuel D. Ingham
  Louis McLane (from August 8, 1831)
- **WAR** – John H. Eaton
  Lewis Cass (from August 8, 1831)
- **NAVY** – John Branch
  Levi Woodbury (from May 23, 1831)
- **ATTORNEY GENERAL** – John M. Berrien
  Roger B. Taney (from July 20, 1831)

SECOND TERM
MARCH 4, 1833–MARCH 4, 1837

- **STATE** – Edward Livingston
  Louis McLane (from May 29, 1833)
  John Forsyth (from July 1, 1834)
- **TREASURY** – Louis McLane
  William J. Duane (from June 1, 1833)
  Roger B. Taney (from September 23, 1833)
  Levi Woodbury (from July 1, 1834)
- **WAR** – Lewis Cass
- **NAVY** – Levi Woodbury
  Mahlon Dickerson (from June 30 ,1834)
- **ATTORNEY GENERAL** – Roger B. Taney
  Benjamin F. Butler (from November 18, 1833)

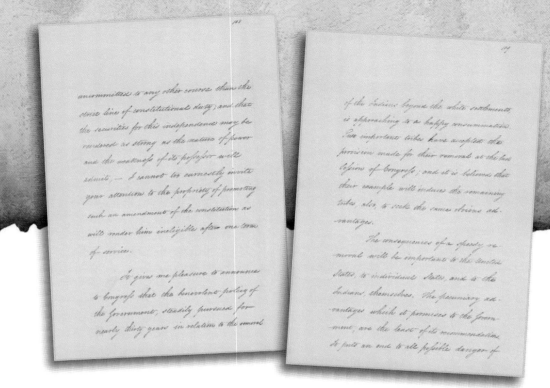

While Jackson was president, relations with Native Americans were challenging. Cherokee, Seminole, and other Native American tribes were losing more and more land.

In 1829, Georgia took over land that the United States had guaranteed to the Cherokee. The U.S. **Supreme Court** ruled against Georgia's actions. However, Jackson did not enforce the ruling.

Instead, Jackson signed the Indian Removal Act of 1830. It stated that all Native Americans had to move west of the Mississippi River. Eight years later, 15,000 Cherokee were forced to move west. Nearly one-quarter of them died. This tragedy became known as the Trail of Tears.

Meanwhile, President Jackson and Vice President Calhoun disagreed about the **Tariff** of Abominations. It placed high taxes on foreign goods.

President Adams had passed the tariff in 1828 to protect Northern businesses. Jackson supported it. But Calhoun felt it was unfair to the South. His home state of South Carolina was especially upset.

In 1832, South Carolina passed the Ordinance of Nullification. This stated that it would ignore the tariff. The state also threatened to **secede** if the U.S. government interfered.

Jackson felt South Carolina was abusing its rights by ignoring the federal government. He feared the United States would break apart. At the end of the year, Calhoun resigned because of the disagreement.

The following year, Kentucky senator Henry Clay proposed two bills as a solution. The first one lessened the tariff. The second was the Force Bill. It allowed the president to use the military to enforce national laws. Clay's bills helped keep the nation united.

In the meantime, Jackson had been focusing on his reelection. The Bank of the United States was set to expire in 1836. So in 1832, Congress approved a bill to renew it. Jackson believed the bank would hurt America's businesses. So, he **vetoed** the bill. The bank then became a main issue during the reelection campaign.

Many voters supported Jackson's stand on the bank. So, he easily won the election with 219 electoral votes. His opponent, Senator Clay, received 49 electoral votes. Martin Van Buren became Jackson's new vice president.

In Jackson's second term, he openly opposed the Bank of the United States. He removed federal funds from the bank. Then, he put the money in state banks instead. Congress felt Jackson's actions were **unconstitutional**. So, the Senate voted to **censure** the president.

During his two terms, President Jackson often disagreed with Congress. He vetoed more bills than any president before him. This gave more power to the presidency. Jackson felt that the president best represents the voice of the people.

SUPREME COURT APPOINTMENTS

JOHN McLEAN - 1830
HENRY BALDWIN - 1830
JAMES M. WAYNE - 1835
ROGER B. TANEY - 1836
PHILIP P. BARBOUR - 1836

President Jackson defeated Senator Clay by more than 200,000 popular votes in the 1832 election.

FINAL YEARS

President Jackson did not run for a third term. On March 4, 1837, Van Buren was **inaugurated** the eighth U.S. president. Jackson then retired to the Hermitage. He was 69 years old.

Jackson had been ill for many years. He had **tuberculosis** and had lost his sight in his right eye. In addition, Jackson still ached from old wounds.

Yet Jackson remained active. He watched over his plantation and received many visitors. Jackson also stayed active in the **Democratic** Party.

Jackson's actions influenced politics for many years after his presidency.

He supported Van Buren for reelection in 1840. In 1844, he supported **Democrat** James K. Polk for president.

On June 8, 1845, Andrew Jackson died. He was buried at the Hermitage next to his wife, Rachel. Jackson is remembered as a tough leader. He stood up for the common man. Jackson fought for what he felt was best for the American people.

Martin Van Buren was Jackson's secretary of state and then his vice president. From 1837 to 1841, Van Buren served as U.S. president.

OFFICE OF THE PRESIDENT

BRANCHES OF GOVERNMENT

The U.S. government is divided into three branches. They are the executive, legislative, and judicial branches. This division is called a separation of powers. Each branch has some power over the others. This is called a system of checks and balances.

EXECUTIVE BRANCH

The executive branch enforces laws. It is made up of the president, the vice president, and the president's cabinet. The president represents the United States around the world. He or she oversees relations with other countries and signs treaties. The president signs bills into law and appoints officials and federal judges. He or she also leads the military and manages government workers.

LEGISLATIVE BRANCH

The legislative branch makes laws, maintains the military, and regulates trade. It also has the power to declare war. This branch consists of the Senate and the House of Representatives. Together, these two houses make up Congress. Each state has two senators. A state's population determines the number of representatives it has.

JUDICIAL BRANCH

The judicial branch interprets laws. It consists of district courts, courts of appeals, and the Supreme Court. District courts try cases. If a person disagrees with a trial's outcome, he or she may appeal. If the courts of appeals support the ruling, a person may appeal to the Supreme Court. The Supreme Court also makes sure that laws follow the U.S. Constitution.

QUALIFICATIONS FOR OFFICE

To be president, a person must meet three requirements. A candidate must be at least 35 years old and a natural-born U.S. citizen. He or she must also have lived in the United States for at least 14 years.

ELECTORAL COLLEGE

The U.S. presidential election is an indirect election. Voters from each state choose electors to represent them in the Electoral College. The number of electors from each state is based on population. Each elector has one electoral vote. Electors are pledged to cast their vote for the candidate who receives the highest number of popular votes in their state. A candidate must receive the majority of Electoral College votes to win.

TERM OF OFFICE

Each president may be elected to two four-year terms. Sometimes, a president may only be elected once. This happens if he or she served more than two years of the previous president's term.

The presidential election is held on the Tuesday after the first Monday in November. The president is sworn in on January 20 of the following year. At that time, he or she takes the oath of office:

I do solemnly swear (or affirm) that I will faithfully execute the office of President of the United States, and will to the best of my ability, preserve, protect and defend the Constitution of the United States.

LINE OF SUCCESSION

The Presidential Succession Act of 1947 defines who becomes president if the president cannot serve. The vice president is first in the line of succession. Next are the Speaker of the House and the President Pro Tempore of the Senate. If none of these individuals is able to serve, the office falls to the president's cabinet members. They would take office in the order in which each department was created:

| Secretary of State |
| Secretary of the Treasury |
| Secretary of Defense |
| Attorney General |
| Secretary of the Interior |
| Secretary of Agriculture |
| Secretary of Commerce |
| Secretary of Labor |
| Secretary of Health and Human Services |
| Secretary of Housing and Urban Development |
| Secretary of Transportation |
| Secretary of Energy |
| Secretary of Education |
| Secretary of Veterans Affairs |
| Secretary of Homeland Security |

BENEFITS

• While in office, the president receives a salary of $400,000 each year. He or she lives in the White House and has 24-hour Secret Service protection.

• The president may travel on a Boeing 747 jet called Air Force One. The airplane can accommodate 70 passengers. It has kitchens, a dining room, sleeping areas, and a conference room. It also has fully equipped offices with the latest communications systems. Air Force One can fly halfway around the world before needing to refuel. It can even refuel in flight!

• If the president wishes to travel by car, he or she uses Cadillac One. Cadillac One is a Cadillac Deville. It has been modified with heavy armor and communications systems. The president takes Cadillac One along when visiting other countries if secure transportation will be needed.

• The president also travels on a helicopter called Marine One. Like the presidential car, Marine One accompanies the president when traveling abroad if necessary.

• Sometimes, the president needs to get away and relax with family and friends. Camp David is the official presidential retreat. It is located in the cool, wooded mountains in Maryland. The U.S. Navy maintains the retreat, and the U.S. Marine Corps keeps it secure. The camp offers swimming, tennis, golf, and hiking.

• When the president leaves office, he or she receives Secret Service protection for ten more years. He or she also receives a yearly pension of $191,300 and funding for office space, supplies, and staff.

PRESIDENTS AND THEIR TERMS

PRESIDENT	PARTY	TOOK OFFICE	LEFT OFFICE	TERMS SERVED	VICE PRESIDENT
George Washington	None	April 30, 1789	March 4, 1797	Two	John Adams
John Adams	Federalist	March 4, 1797	March 4, 1801	One	Thomas Jefferson
Thomas Jefferson	Democratic-Republican	March 4, 1801	March 4, 1809	Two	Aaron Burr, George Clinton
James Madison	Democratic-Republican	March 4, 1809	March 4, 1817	Two	George Clinton, Elbridge Gerry
James Monroe	Democratic-Republican	March 4, 1817	March 4, 1825	Two	Daniel D. Tompkins
John Quincy Adams	Democratic-Republican	March 4, 1825	March 4, 1829	One	John C. Calhoun
Andrew Jackson	Democrat	March 4, 1829	March 4, 1837	Two	John C. Calhoun, Martin Van Buren
Martin Van Buren	Democrat	March 4, 1837	March 4, 1841	One	Richard M. Johnson
William H. Harrison	Whig	March 4, 1841	April 4, 1841	Died During First Term	John Tyler
John Tyler	Whig	April 6, 1841	March 4, 1845	Completed Harrison's Term	Office Vacant
James K. Polk	Democrat	March 4, 1845	March 4, 1849	One	George M. Dallas
Zachary Taylor	Whig	March 5, 1849	July 9, 1850	Died During First Term	Millard Fillmore

PRESIDENT	PARTY	TOOK OFFICE	LEFT OFFICE	TERMS SERVED	VICE PRESIDENT
Millard Fillmore	Whig	July 10, 1850	March 4, 1853	Completed Taylor's Term	Office Vacant
Franklin Pierce	Democrat	March 4, 1853	March 4, 1857	One	William R.D. King
James Buchanan	Democrat	March 4, 1857	March 4, 1861	One	John C. Breckinridge
Abraham Lincoln	Republican	March 4, 1861	April 15, 1865	Served One Term, Died During Second Term	Hannibal Hamlin, Andrew Johnson
Andrew Johnson	Democrat	April 15, 1865	March 4, 1869	Completed Lincoln's Second Term	Office Vacant
Ulysses S. Grant	Republican	March 4, 1869	March 4, 1877	Two	Schuyler Colfax, Henry Wilson
Rutherford B. Hayes	Republican	March 3, 1877	March 4, 1881	One	William A. Wheeler
James A. Garfield	Republican	March 4, 1881	September 19, 1881	Died During First Term	Chester Arthur
Chester Arthur	Republican	September 20, 1881	March 4, 1885	Completed Garfield's Term	Office Vacant
Grover Cleveland	Democrat	March 4, 1885	March 4, 1889	One	Thomas A. Hendricks
Benjamin Harrison	Republican	March 4, 1889	March 4, 1893	One	Levi P. Morton
Grover Cleveland	Democrat	March 4, 1893	March 4, 1897	One	Adlai E. Stevenson
William McKinley	Republican	March 4, 1897	September 14, 1901	Served One Term, Died During Second Term	Garret A. Hobart, Theodore Roosevelt

PRESIDENT	PARTY	TOOK OFFICE	LEFT OFFICE	TERMS SERVED	VICE PRESIDENT
Theodore Roosevelt	Republican	September 14, 1901	March 4, 1909	Completed McKinley's Second Term, Served One Term	Office Vacant, Charles Fairbanks
William Taft	Republican	March 4, 1909	March 4, 1913	One	James S. Sherman
Woodrow Wilson	Democrat	March 4, 1913	March 4, 1921	Two	Thomas R. Marshall
Warren G. Harding	Republican	March 4, 1921	August 2, 1923	Died During First Term	Calvin Coolidge
Calvin Coolidge	Republican	August 3, 1923	March 4, 1929	Completed Harding's Term, Served One Term	Office Vacant, Charles Dawes
Herbert Hoover	Republican	March 4, 1929	March 4, 1933	One	Charles Curtis
Franklin D. Roosevelt	Democrat	March 4, 1933	April 12, 1945	Served Three Terms, Died During Fourth Term	John Nance Garner, Henry A. Wallace, Harry S. Truman
Harry S. Truman	Democrat	April 12, 1945	January 20, 1953	Completed Roosevelt's Fourth Term, Served One Term	Office Vacant, Alben Barkley
Dwight D. Eisenhower	Republican	January 20, 1953	January 20, 1961	Two	Richard Nixon
John F. Kennedy	Democrat	January 20, 1961	November 22, 1963	Died During First Term	Lyndon B. Johnson
Lyndon B. Johnson	Democrat	November 22, 1963	January 20, 1969	Completed Kennedy's Term, Served One Term	Office Vacant, Hubert H. Humphrey
Richard Nixon	Republican	January 20, 1969	August 9, 1974	Completed First Term, Resigned During Second Term	Spiro T. Agnew, Gerald Ford

PRESIDENT	PARTY	TOOK OFFICE	LEFT OFFICE	TERMS SERVED	VICE PRESIDENT
Gerald Ford	Republican	August 9, 1974	January 20, 1977	Completed Nixon's Second Term	Nelson A. Rockefeller
Jimmy Carter	Democrat	January 20, 1977	January 20, 1981	One	Walter Mondale
Ronald Reagan	Republican	January 20, 1981	January 20, 1989	Two	George H.W. Bush
George H.W. Bush	Republican	January 20, 1989	January 20, 1993	One	Dan Quayle
Bill Clinton	Democrat	January 20, 1993	January 20, 2001	Two	Al Gore
George W. Bush	Republican	January 20, 2001	January 20, 2009	Two	Dick Cheney
Barack Obama	Democrat	January 20, 2009			Joe Biden

"It is to be regretted that the rich and powerful too often bend the acts of government to their selfish purposes." Andrew Jackson

WRITE TO THE PRESIDENT

You may write to the president at:

**The White House
1600 Pennsylvania Avenue NW
Washington, DC 20500**

You may e-mail the president at:

comments@whitehouse.gov

GLOSSARY

American Revolution - from 1775 to 1783. A war for independence between Great Britain and its North American colonies. The colonists won and created the United States of America.

cabinet - a group of advisers chosen by the president to lead government departments.

censure (SEHNT-shuhr) - to officially express disapproval.

cholera - a disease of the intestines that includes severe diarrhea.

constitution - the laws that govern a country or a state.

democracy - a governmental system in which individuals or elected representatives vote on how to run their country.

Democrat - a member of the Democratic political party. When Andrew Jackson was president, Democrats supported farmers and landowners.

duel - a formal fight between two people using weapons in the presence of witnesses.

inaugurate (ih-NAW-gyuh-rayt) - to swear into a political office.

militia (muh-LIH-shuh) - a group of citizens trained for war or emergencies.

secede - to break away from a group.

secretary of state - a member of the president's cabinet who handles relations with other countries.

smallpox - a contagious disease marked by a fever and blisters on the skin. The blisters often leave permanent scars shaped like little pits.

Supreme Court - the highest, most powerful court of a nation or a state.

tariff - the taxes a government puts on imported or exported goods.

tuberculosis - a disease that affects the lungs.

unconstitutional - something that goes against the laws of a constitution.

veto - the right of one member of a decision-making group to stop an action by the group. In the U.S. government, the president can veto bills passed by Congress. But Congress can override the president's veto if two-thirds of its members vote to do so.

War of 1812 - from 1812 to 1814. A war fought between the United States and Great Britain over shipping rights and the capture of U.S. soldiers.

WEB SITES

To learn more about Andrew Jackson, visit ABDO Publishing Company on the World Wide Web at **www.abdopublishing.com**. Web sites about Andrew Jackson are featured on our Book Links page. These links are routinely monitored and updated to provide the most current information available.

INDEX